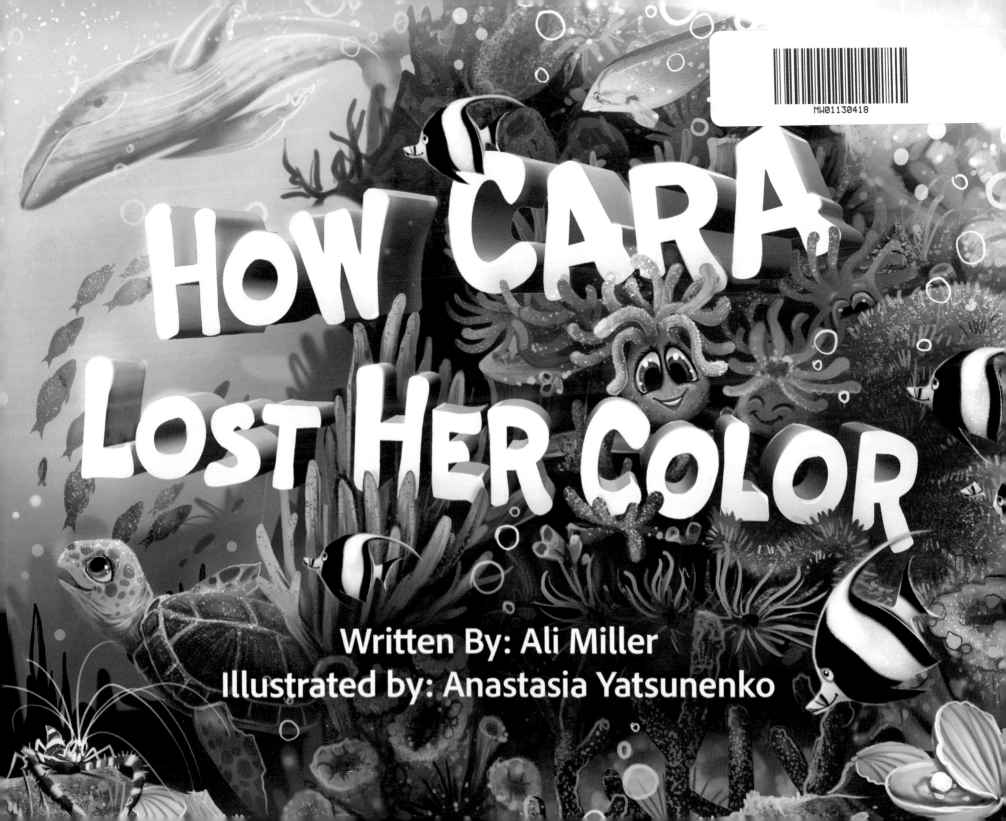

How Cara Lost Her Color

Written By: Ali Miller

Illustrated by: Anastasia Yatsunenko

Edited by: Kristen Forbes
Illustrated by: Anastasia Yatsunenko

ISBN: 978-1-7338815-1-7

Dedications

This book is dedicated to my niece, Kaylee Marie, and nephew, Noah Lee. My greatest wish is that they will be able to experience the beauty of coral reefs when they grow up.

Acknowledgements

I would like to thank the following individuals and organizations for their inspiration and support:

My family, for always supporting me in everything I do, even if that means moving 2,500 miles away to study marine life. They have always taught me to follow my dreams.

The education department and all of the staff I had the privilege of working with at the Maui Ocean Center Aquarium. I am truly grateful for the time I spent working as a marine naturalist. It was a dream to teach guests from all over the world about the importance of Hawaii's coral reef ecosystems and unique marine animals. The employees at the Maui Ocean Center are some of the most dedicated and inspirational people I've ever met.

My instructors—Donna Brown, Dr. Meagan Jones, Darla White, and Tim Botkin— at the University of Hawaii Maui College. Each one of them showed me a unique perspective on the complex relationship between coral reefs and climate change. Without them, this book would not exist.

Dr. Sylvia Earle, for all of her contributions to marine science and ocean conservation during her career. Her work is invaluable, and her passion for protecting the ocean has inspired many people. She is a visionary, a pioneer, and truly a role model for humanity.

Author's Note

Over the past several decades, global carbon emissions have led to warming ocean temperatures. As greenhouse gasses—like carbon dioxide—trap heat inside the atmosphere, the planet warms, and the ocean absorbs much of that heat. Corals are sensitive to temperature and many respond to heat stress by releasing the symbiotic algae that lives in their tissues. This is known as "coral bleaching." Unless atmospheric carbon emissions are reduced, the survival of these vital marine ecosystems is at risk. Let's work together to save the reefs!

New Words

<u>Algae</u> (like Zoey) are very tiny plant-like creatures that live in the ocean and use the sun to make their own food.

<u>Corals</u> are tiny animals related to jellyfish that live in groups called "colonies." They build their own skeletons, creating large areas of coral reefs and providing homes for lots of different ocean animals. Many corals have a special type of algae living in their bodies that use sunlight to make food.

<u>Coral bleaching</u> happens when polyps lose their algae partners due to heat or stress, causing them to turn white. A **polyp** is a single coral animal. Each polyp has a mouth and sticky tentacles which it uses to catch food.

<u>Grief</u> means lots of sadness.

<u>Plankton</u> are tiny creatures floating in the ocean. Some will grow up to become fish, sea stars, or snails, but some will stay tiny their entire lives.

<u>Temperature</u> measures how hot or cold something is.

<u>Tides</u> are the rise and fall of the levels of the ocean. They are caused by the gravitational pull of the Sun and Moon.

<u>Seaweeds</u> are large algae, much like ocean plants.

A **species** is a distinct group of plants or animals that have common characteristics.

Far away from man,
south in the Pacific,

there lives a small coral polyp
and a huge family she grew up with.

Hundreds and hundreds of tiny little creatures
with little tiny mouths and sticky arm-like features.

They share a skeleton made of minerals like stone.
They make it themselves—strong like human bone!

Attached to the reef, they all share a home
with a special type of algae that helps them to grow!

Cara is the brightest polyp
and Zoey is her best friend.

Cara gives Zoey's family a home,
while their garden feeds Cara for days on end.

Cara and her algae friend live together in peace,
along with their families and other friends on the reef.

Her beautiful pink color
comes from the little algae inside.

Everyone takes care of each other
as they laugh each day away with the tide.

"Good morning, little Zoey! How's the garden today?"

"It's looking wonderful, Cara! I know you like your food this way."

But when humans moved to the islands nearby,
the temperature in the ocean started to rise.

One hot summer day, Cara said to Zoey,

"It's feeling very warm, my friend. How's the garden doing?"

Zoey replied, "Yes indeed, it's hotter than ever this summer!"

"The garden is still growing for now, but you're looking weaker, Cara!"

Within weeks the temperature rose so high that Zoey's family had to flee,
leaving their polyp friends behind without a garden to feed the reef.

"Goodbye for now, Cara. I'll miss you so much!"
"I wish you all could come with me!"

"Oh little Zoey, I wish we could too,
but my family's bones are stuck to the reef!"

Zoey left with her family and Cara couldn't help but cry
as she looked around at her home.

The reef was turning white and her parents were sick.
Without Zoey's family, nothing could grow.

The algae gave the reef its color, all different shades and hues.
Now that Cara's friends had left, she didn't have a garden of food.

When Cara's family got weaker,
she tried catching plankton with her arms.

She had to work hard to get food,
and make sure no one would starve!

As more of the corals started bleaching white,
the bad kind of seaweed crept up at night.

It was slowly growing during each day,
sneaking up closer to where Cara stayed.

When humans finally looked down at the reef,
each one of their hearts quickly filled up with grief.

They wanted to make a change. It became their greatest wish.
They knew it was the only way to bring back all the fish.

The temperature dropped to normal
as summer came to an end.

Everything started to cool down,
and the bad seaweed finally shed.

Within a short time, Zoey's family came back,
and everyone lit up with glee!

The reef had its color, and the fish had returned,
bringing balance back to the changing sea.

"Oh little Zoey, I missed you so much!"

"I didn't know what I should do!"

"Oh my dear Cara, I'm so happy we're back!"

"My home will always be with you!"

When the humans above started changing their ways,

Zoey and her family were finally able to stay...

Living in harmony with the corals, fish, and other species
that all work together to take care of the reef.

The End.

The Author

Ali Miller grew up in Reno, Nevada, where she studied psychology at Truckee Meadows Community College. She has always been fascinated by the ocean and passionate about marine conservation. She moved to Maui—the second largest of the Hawaiian Islands— in 2015 after her first experience snorkeling around Hawaii's coral reefs. She spent four years studying marine biology and sustainable science management at the University of Hawaii Maui College. At the Maui Ocean Center (Maui's aquarium), Ali enjoyed working as a marine naturalist for two years in the education department. At the aquarium, she was able to educate guests from around the world about the importance of Hawaii's unique coral reef ecosystems. She plans to write more books and to continue introducing new scientific concepts to young children.

The Illustrator

Anastasia Yatsunenko is an artist and illustrator from the city of Kiev, Ukraine. She has always thought of the ocean as an unexplored universe, and although she grew up far away from the water, she loved visiting the beach with her parents as a child. Anastasia spent five years studying graphic design at Kiev National University of Culture and Arts. She plans to continue illustrating, travelling, and spending more time near the sea. While illustrating this book and bringing Cara and Zoey to life, she enjoyed learning many new things about coral.